"Master the Ladder: The Proven Blueprint for Career Growth"

Effective Step-by-Step Strategies for Success

By
Ameerayy Ali

Contents

Preface 1
Reader's Guide 2
Introduction: Navigating Your Career Journey 4
Chapter 1: Setting the Stage – Crafting Your Unique Career Strategy 6
Worksheet for Chapter 1: Setting the Stage – Crafting Your Unique Career Strategy 12
Chapter 2: Mastering the Art of Goal Setting 15
Worksheet for Chapter 2: Identifying Your Strengths and Weaknesses 21
Chapter 3: Leveraging Reflection and Feedback for Personal and Professional Growth 25
Worksheet for Chapter 3: Building a Personal Brand 32
Chapter 4: The Balance of Ambition and Contentment ... 37
Worksheet for Chapter 4: Overcoming Setbacks with Integrity and Resilience 45
Chapter 5: Staying Motivated – Managing Stress and Building Resilience 50
Worksheet for Chapter 5: Building and Leveraging a Powerful Network 57
Chapter 6: Navigating Career Transitions – Planning Your Next Move 62
Worksheet for Chapter 6: Navigating Career Transitions – Planning Your Next Move 69
Chapter 7: Navigating Office Politics and Digital Dynamics 73

Worksheet for Chapter 7: Building and Leveraging Your Professional Network 79

Chapter 8: Never stop learning! Stay ahead of the game. 84

Worksheet for Chapter 8: Continuous Learning and Staying Ahead of the Curve 89

Chapter 9: Balancing Work and Life – Maximizing Productivity 94

Worksheet for Chapter 9: Balancing Work and Life – Maximizing Productivity 102

Chapter 10: Measuring Progress and Building Your Career Legacy 107

Worksheet for Chapter 10: Building a Lasting Legacy – Making an Impact That Endures 112

Preface

When I began my career, I thought success was a straightforward climb up a ladder. However, over the years, I realized that the path to career fulfillment is much more nuanced and personal. It's not just about reaching the top—it's about understanding where you want to go, leveraging your unique strengths, and navigating the inevitable challenges along the way with integrity and resilience.

"Master the Ladder: A Strategic Blueprint for Success" is the culmination of insights gathered from my own career journey and from helping countless professionals like you. This book is designed to provide you with the tools and strategies that will empower you to take control of your career path, no matter where you are starting from. Whether you are looking to advance to the next level, pivot to a new field, or simply find more fulfillment in your current role, this book will serve as your roadmap.

My goal with this book is to help you craft a career that is not only successful but also meaningful. I hope the strategies, case studies, and exercises in this book inspire you to take bold steps in your career while staying true to your values and personal goals.

Reader's Guide

This book is structured to meet you where you are in your career journey. Depending on your current needs, you might find some chapters more immediately relevant than others. Here's a quick guide on how to navigate the book based on common career scenarios:

- If You're Just Starting Out:
Begin with Chapter 1, Setting the Stage – Crafting Your Unique Career Strategy, to establish a strong foundation for your career.

If You're Defining Your Unique Value:
Head to Chapter 2, Identifying and Leveraging Your Unique Value Proposition, will help you uncover and articulate what makes you stand out in your field.

If You're Building Relationships and Expanding Your Network:
Head to Chapter 3, Building and Nurturing Professional Relationships where you will Learn effective networking strategies, both online and offline that can open doors and accelerate your career growth.

- If You're Facing Setbacks or Challenges:
Head to Chapter 4, Overcoming Setbacks with Integrity and Resilience, for strategies on bouncing back stronger.

- If You're Managing Stress and Staying Motivated:
Head to Chapter 5, Staying Motivated – Managing Stress and Building Resilience, where we will provide you with stress management techniques and motivation strategies to help you maintain your drive and focus.

- If You're Focused on Growth and Advancement:
Chapter 6, Navigating Career Transitions – Planning Your Next Move, will provide you with tools to make strategic decisions.

- If You're Navigating Office Politics and Digital Dynamics:
Turn to Chapter 7, Navigating Office Politics and Digital Dynamics, for insights on handling the complex world of office politics and the impact of digital communication on workplace relationships.

- If You're Continuously Learning:
Chapter 8, Continuous Learning and Staying Ahead of the Curve, will guide you on how to keep your skills sharp and stay relevant in your industry.

- If You're Balancing Career and Personal Life:
Chapter 9, Balancing Work and Life – Maximizing Productivity, offers tips on maintaining a healthy equilibrium while progressing in your career.

- If You're Measuring Success and Building a Legacy:
Conclude your journey with Chapter 10, Measuring Progress and Building Your Career Legacy, where you'll learn how to track your achievements, define success on your terms, and create a lasting impact in your career and beyond.

Feel free to skip around as needed, and don't hesitate to revisit chapters as your career evolves. The exercises and tools provided are designed to be revisited and adapted as you grow.

Introduction: Navigating Your Career Journey

In today's fast-paced world, the path to career success is more complex than ever before. Whether you are a seasoned professional looking to advance to the next level or someone just starting out, navigating your career requires a blend of strategy, emotional intelligence, and continuous growth. This book, Master the Ladder: A Strategic Blueprint for Success, is designed to be your comprehensive guide through the various stages of your career, offering practical tools and strategies that are easy to implement in real-time.

A fulfilling career is like a treasure hunt, with clues leading you in unexpected directions. It's a dynamic process that requires adapting to new challenges, seizing opportunities, and continuously reassessing your goals. This book is structured to reflect that complexity, with each chapter offering actionable insights into different aspects of your professional life. You don't have to read it cover-to-cover—feel free to jump to the sections that resonate most with your current situation.

We understand that as a busy professional, time is your most valuable asset. That's why this book is designed to deliver high-impact advice in a concise, accessible format. Each chapter is packed with practical exercises, case studies, and quick wins that you can start implementing immediately. Additionally, to deepen your understanding and help you apply the concepts more thoroughly, each chapter concludes with a worksheet. These worksheets are crafted to guide you in reflecting on the chapter's key lessons, setting clear goals, and planning actionable steps tailored to your unique situation.

By taking the time to complete these worksheets, you will not only reinforce the knowledge you've gained but also transform it into tangible progress in your career. Whether you're refining your career strategy, building resilience, or managing work-life balance, the tools and techniques provided here will help you master your career ladder with confidence and purpose.

Chapter 1: Setting the Stage – Crafting Your Unique Career Strategy

When embarking on any significant journey, it's crucial to know your destination. In your career, that destination is defined by your goals and the vision you have for your professional life. However, before you can start climbing the ladder, you must first build a solid foundation. This chapter will guide you through the essential steps to create a personalized career strategy that aligns with your strengths, values, and long-term aspirations.

Understanding Career Foundations

A well-constructed career strategy begins with a deep understanding of what you want from your career. This may seem straightforward, but many professionals struggle with identifying their true desires and aspirations. They may find themselves pursuing paths defined by societal expectations, family pressures, or the allure of a high salary, only to discover later that their careers lack meaning or satisfaction.

To avoid this pitfall, it's important to take the time to reflect on what truly matters to you. What gets your engine running in the morning? What kind of work makes your heart sing? What values do you hold dear, and how can your career align with them? These questions are fundamental in defining your career's foundation.

Start by writing down your core values. These might include integrity, creativity, helping others, or continuous learning. Once you've identified these values, consider how they can be integrated into your career. For example, if creativity is a core value, you might seek roles that allow you to innovate and think outside the box. If helping others is important to you, you might look for opportunities in industries like healthcare, education, or social services.

By grounding your career in your values, you create a foundation that not only supports your professional growth but also ensures that your work is meaningful and aligned with your personal beliefs.

Strengths Identification

Once you've established your career's foundation, the next step is to identify your strengths. Understanding what you do best is key to crafting a career strategy that plays to your strengths, allowing you to excel and find satisfaction in your work.

There are several tools available to help you identify your strengths, but one of the most widely used is the CliftonStrengths assessment (formerly known as StrengthsFinder). This tool helps you discover your top strengths, or "talents," which are innate ways of thinking, feeling, and behaving. By focusing on these strengths, you can leverage them to achieve your career goals more effectively.

Here's a step-by-step guide on how to use a strengths assessment tool like CliftonStrengths:

1. **Take the Assessment**: Set aside about 30 minutes to complete the assessment. Answer the questions honestly and quickly, going with your initial instinct rather than overthinking your responses.
2. **Review Your Results**: After completing the assessment, you'll receive a report detailing your top strengths. Take the time to read through each strength description carefully. Reflect on how these strengths have shown up in your career so far.
3. **Identify Patterns**: Look for patterns in your strengths. For example, if several of your top strengths are related to communication, this might suggest that roles requiring strong interpersonal

skills, such as sales, public relations, or teaching, would be a good fit for you.
4. **Apply Your Strengths**: Once you've identified your strengths, think about how you can apply them in your current role. Are there tasks or projects that align with your strengths? If so, seek out opportunities to get involved in these areas.
5. **Communicate Your Strengths**: Finally, make sure to communicate your strengths to others, especially in job interviews, performance reviews, and networking situations. Knowing and articulating your strengths can set you apart from others and position you as a valuable asset to any team or organization.

Strengths identification is not just about recognizing what you're good at; it's about strategically aligning your career with these strengths to maximize your potential and achieve greater satisfaction in your work.

Crafting a Career Vision

With a solid understanding of your values and strengths, you're now ready to craft a vision for your career. A career vision is a clear, compelling statement of what you want to achieve in your professional life. It serves as a North Star, guiding your decisions and actions as you progress along your career path.
Creating a career vision begins with setting long-term goals. Think about where you want to be in 5, 10, or even 20 years. What roles do you aspire to? What kind of impact do you want to make? Consider both your personal aspirations and the broader contributions you want to make to your industry or society.

Here are some steps to help you craft a career vision:

1. **Dream Big:** Don't limit yourself by thinking only about what seems achievable in the short term. Allow yourself to dream big and imagine the ideal scenario for your career. What would your perfect job look like? What kind of environment would you work in? Who would you work with?
2. **Write a Vision Statement**: Once you've identified your aspirations, distill them into a clear, concise vision statement. For example, "I want to become a leading expert in sustainable energy, helping to develop innovative solutions that combat climate change."
3. **Break Down Your Vision**: After defining your vision, break it down into smaller, actionable goals. For example, if your vision is to become a leading expert in sustainable energy, you might set goals such as earning an advanced degree in environmental science, gaining experience in renewable energy projects, or building a professional network in the sustainability sector.
4. **Align Your Vision with Your Values and Strengths**: Make sure your vision aligns with the values and strengths you identified earlier. A vision that resonates with your core beliefs and leverages your natural talents will be more motivating and sustainable in the long run.
5. **Revisit and Refine Your Vision**: Your career vision may evolve over time as you gain more experience and your interests change. Revisit and refine your vision periodically to ensure it remains relevant and inspiring.

Crafting a career vision is a powerful exercise that helps you clarify your direction and purpose. It provides a sense of focus and motivation, ensuring that your daily actions contribute to your long-term goals.

Quick Wins

Now that you have a foundation in place with a clear understanding of your values, strengths, and career vision, it's time to start taking action. Here are some quick wins to help you begin aligning your daily work with your long-term career goals:

1. **Set Daily Intentions**: At the start of each day, take a few minutes to set an intention that aligns with your career vision. For example, if your goal is to develop leadership skills, your daily intention might be to take on a leadership role in a meeting or to mentor a junior colleague.
2. **Seek Feedback**: Actively seek feedback from colleagues and supervisors on how well you are applying your strengths in your current role. Use this feedback to identify areas for improvement and to find new ways to leverage your strengths.
3. **Identify Opportunities for Growth**: Look for opportunities within your current role to grow and develop. This could be taking on a new project, learning a new skill, or volunteering for a cross-functional team.
4. **Network with Purpose**: Begin building a network of professionals who align with your career vision. Attend industry events, join professional organizations, and connect with like-minded individuals on LinkedIn.
5. **Reflect and Adjust**: At the end of each week, reflect on your progress. What actions did you take that aligned with your career vision? What challenges did you encounter, and how can you overcome them moving forward? Use these reflections to adjust your strategy as needed.

These quick wins are designed to help you start making immediate progress toward your career goals. By consistently taking small, purposeful actions, you'll begin to see significant momentum in your career.

Conclusion

Setting the stage for your career involves more than just setting goals; it's about creating a strategy that is deeply rooted in your values, strengths, and long-term vision. By taking the time to understand what drives you, identifying your unique talents, and crafting a clear career vision, you lay the groundwork for a successful and fulfilling professional journey.
Remember, your career is a marathon, not a sprint. The steps you take today will have a lasting impact on your future. As you move forward, keep revisiting the foundation you've built in this chapter. Stay true to your values, continue to leverage your strengths, and refine your vision as you grow. With a solid foundation in place, you're well on your way to mastering the ladder of success.

Worksheet for Chapter 1: Setting the Stage – Crafting Your Unique Career Strategy

A. Reflection

1. **What are your core values, and how do they influence your career choices?**
    - _____
    - _____
    - _____

2. **How does your current career align with your long-term aspirations?**
    - _____
    - _____
    - _____

3. **What skills or experiences have been most valuable to you so far?**
    - _____
    - _____
    - _____

B. Application

1. **Identify three strengths that will help you craft your career strategy:**
    - Strength 1:
      _____
      _____
    - Strength 2:
      _____
      _____

- Strength 3:
  _____
  _____

2. **List two areas where you need further development to achieve your career goals:**
   - Development Area 1:
     _____
     _____
   - Development Area 2:
     _____
     _____

3. **Who can you collaborate with to enhance your career strategy? List potential mentors, peers, or resources.**
   - _____
   - _____
   - _____

C. Planning with CLEAR Goals

1. **Collaborative:** Who will you involve in your career planning process?
   - _____
   - _____

2. **Limited:** What are the specific and manageable career milestones you want to achieve in the next six months?
   - _____
   - _____

3. **Emotional:** Why is achieving these career milestones important to you on a personal level?
   - _____

o _____

4. **Appreciable:** What small steps can you take right now to move closer to your career goals?
   o Step 1:
   _____
   _____

   o Step 2:
   _____
   _____

   o Step 3:
   _____
   _____

5. **Refinable:** How will you adapt your goals if circumstances change or new opportunities arise?
   o _____
   o _____
   o _____

D. Progress Tracking

1. **Check-In:** How is your career strategy evolving? Reflect on your progress every month.
   o _____
   o _____
   o

2. **Adjustments:** What adjustments do you need to make to stay on track or refine your strategy?
   o _____
   o _____
   o _____

Chapter 2: Mastering the Art of Goal Setting

There's more to goal setting than just determining what you want to accomplish. It's about laying the groundwork for success and creating a path that leads you from where you are to where you want to be. In the ever-evolving landscape of personal and professional development, a new approach to goal setting is emerging—one that is more flexible, human-centered, and better suited for today's rapidly changing world.

This chapter introduces the **CLEAR goals framework**, a modern take on goal setting that emphasizes continuous learning, agility, and relevance in achieving meaningful success.

The CLEAR Goals Framework

CLEAR is an acronym for **Collaborative, Limited, Emotional, Appreciable, and Refinable.** This approach shifts away from the rigidity of traditional goal-setting methods like SMART, offering a more fluid and adaptable structure that resonates with the complexities of modern life.

Let's break down each component of CLEAR goals:

Collaborative: Goals should encourage teamwork and collaboration. In today's interconnected world, very few goals are achieved in isolation. The collaborative aspect of CLEAR goals emphasizes the importance of working with others, leveraging collective strengths, and fostering a supportive environment where success is shared. Example: Instead of setting a goal to "increase personal sales by 20%," a CLEAR goal might be "collaborate with the sales team to increase overall department revenue by 15%." This encourages working together, sharing knowledge, and pooling resources to achieve a common goal.

Limited: Goals should be limited in scope and duration. Instead of setting lofty, long-term goals, CLEAR goals prioritize specific, achievable tasks with short deadlines. This keeps you agile and able to adapt as circumstances change.
Example: Rather than aiming to "become a thought leader in your industry," a more limited goal would be to "write three industry-specific articles over the next three months." This approach breaks down larger ambitions into bite-sized, actionable steps.

Emotional: Goals should tap into your emotions, connecting deeply with your intrinsic motivations. When a goal resonates emotionally, it becomes more meaningful and inspiring, driving you to push through challenges and stay committed even when things get tough.
Example: Instead of setting a goal like "increase client retention by 10%," a CLEAR goal might be "build lasting relationships with clients by understanding their unique needs and providing tailored solutions." This goal addresses the emotional component of trust and value.

Appreciable: Goals should be broken down into smaller, appreciable milestones. Much like building blocks, these smaller steps are easier to achieve and help maintain momentum. Appreciable goals encourage continuous progress and prevent the feeling of being overwhelmed by the size of the task ahead.
Example Think of it like this: If your destination is to launch a new product, a more manageable waypoint might be to finish market research and prototyping by the end of the quarter. By focusing on smaller milestones, you can steadily move toward the larger objective without losing sight of progress.

Refinable: Goals should be flexible and open to refinement. As you progress, new information or changes

in circumstances may require you to adjust your goals. The refinable nature of CLEAR goals allows for this adaptability, ensuring that your goals remain relevant and achievable in a dynamic environment.
Example: If your goal is to "expand into a new market by the end of the year," a refinable goal might be "adjust the expansion strategy based on quarterly market feedback and changing conditions." This adaptability allows you to change course as needed, while staying focused on the main goal.

Implementing CLEAR Goals

Adopting the CLEAR framework involves shifting your mindset from a traditional, static approach to one that is more fluid and responsive to change. Here's how to incorporate CLEAR goals into your daily life:
Start with Collaboration: Identify the stakeholders and collaborators who can help you achieve your goal. Whether its colleagues, mentors, or partners, fostering a spirit of teamwork from the outset will ensure that you're supported and aligned with those who can contribute to your success.

1. **Limit Your Focus:** Narrow your goal down to something that is both manageable and achievable within a reasonable timeframe. Focus on what you can realistically accomplish in the short term, and avoid the temptation to overreach.
2. **Connect Emotionally:** Take a moment to reflect on why this goal matters to you. What intrinsic motivations drive you to achieve this? Does this fit with your beliefs and goals? By connecting emotionally, you'll find the motivation to persevere through challenges.
3. **Break It Down:** Divide your goal into smaller, appreciable steps. Each step should feel like a small victory, moving you closer to the ultimate objective. Celebrate these milestones, as they

provide valuable feedback and keep your momentum going.
4. **Be Ready to Refine:** As you move forward, be open to refining your goals. Things change, priorities shift. Regularly review your progress and make adjustments as needed to ensure that your goals remain relevant and achievable.

Benefits of the CLEAR Framework

The CLEAR framework offers several advantages over more traditional goal-setting methods:
Flexibility: In a world that's constantly changing, flexibility is crucial. CLEAR goals allow you to pivot and adjust your approach as needed, without feeling like you're straying off course.
Collaboration: By emphasizing collaboration, CLEAR goals harness the power of teamwork. This collective effort often leads to better outcomes than individual efforts alone.
Emotional Resonance: Goals that connect with your emotions are more likely to inspire and motivate you. The CLEAR framework encourages you to set goals that are personally meaningful, increasing your chances of success.
Continuous Progress: Breaking goals down into appreciable steps ensures that you're always making progress, even if it's just a small step at a time. This continuous momentum helps prevent stagnation and keeps you moving forward.
Adaptability: Life is unpredictable, and your goals should reflect that reality. The refinable nature of CLEAR goals ensures that you can adapt to changing circumstances without losing sight of your long-term vision.

The CLEAR Mindset: Beyond Goal Setting

Embracing the CLEAR framework requires more than just changing how you set goals—it's about adopting a new mindset. This mindset is one of agility, collaboration, and emotional connection Success is a winding path, not a straight line, filled with unexpected turns and continuous growth.
As you work toward your goals, remember that the path may not always be clear. But with the CLEAR framework, you'll have a robust and flexible approach that allows you to navigate challenges, adapt to new realities, and achieve success in a way that's both meaningful and sustainable.

Quick Wins

1. **Create a Vision Board**: Spend 30 minutes gathering images, quotes, and symbols that represent your life goals. Arrange them on a vision board where you can see them daily.
2. **Define Your Core Values**: Write down your top five core values. Reflect on how these values align with your current goals and daily actions.
3. **Start a Morning Routine**: Design a simple morning routine that includes at least one activity that aligns with your goals, such as journaling, reading, or exercise.
4. **Identify Your Strengths:** Take a personality or strengths assessment to identify your key strengths. Consider how you can leverage these strengths in your goal-setting process.
5. **Set a Mini Goal:** Choose a small, achievable goal that you can complete within the next week. Focus on the process and celebrate your achievement.

Conclusion

The CLEAR goals framework offers a refreshing and adaptive approach to goal setting in today's dynamic environment. By focusing on collaboration, limiting scope, connecting emotionally, breaking down tasks into appreciable steps, and maintaining flexibility, you can create goals that are not only achievable but also deeply resonant with your personal and professional aspirations.

As you move forward, consider how the CLEAR framework can be integrated into your daily life. It's more than just a method-it's a philosophy that encourages growth, adaptability, and sustained progress on your journey to success.

Worksheet for Chapter 2: Identifying Your Strengths and Weaknesses

A. Self-Assessment

1. **List your top five strengths that have positively impacted your career so far:**
   - Strength 1: _____
   - Strength 2: _____
   - Strength 3: _____
   - Strength 4: _____
   - Strength 5: _____

2. **Identify three weaknesses that have held you back in your career:**
   - Weakness 1: _____
   - Weakness 2: _____
   - Weakness 3: _____

3. **Which of your strengths do you feel most proud of? Why?**
   - _____
   - _____
   - _____

4. **How have your weaknesses affected your career progression or opportunities?**
   - _____

AMEERAYY ALI

- o _____
- o _____

B. Feedback from Others

1. **Ask three colleagues or mentors to share what they believe are your top strengths:**
   - o Colleague/Mentor 1:
     _____
   - o Colleague/Mentor 2:
     _____
   - o Colleague/Mentor 3:
     _____

2. **What weaknesses do they perceive in your professional approach?**
   - o Colleague/Mentor 1:
     _____
   - o Colleague/Mentor 2:
     _____
   - o Colleague/Mentor 3:
     _____

3. **How does their feedback compare with your self-assessment?**
   - o _____
   - o _____
   - o _____

C. Planning with CLEAR Goals

1. **Collaborative:** Who can you work with to further develop your strengths?
   - o _____
   - o _____

2. **Limited:** What specific steps can you take to address one of your weaknesses in the next month?
    - Step 1:
      _____
      _____
    - Step 2:
      _____
      _____

3. **Emotional:** Why is it important for you to improve in these areas? How will it impact your career and personal growth?
    - _____
    - _____

4. **Appreciable:** Break down a larger goal into smaller, manageable tasks that you can start working on this week:
    - Task 1:
      _____
      _____
    - Task 2:
      _____
      _____
    - Task 3:
      _____
      _____

5. **Refinable:** How will you refine your approach if you face difficulties in improving your weaknesses?
    - _____
    - _____
    - _____

D. Progress Tracking

1. **Monthly Review:** How have you worked on your strengths and weaknesses this month? Reflect on your progress.
   - _____
   - _____
   - _____

2. **Adjustments:** What changes will you make to your plan based on what you've learned?
   - _____
   - _____
   - _____

Chapter 3: Leveraging Reflection and Feedback for Personal and Professional Growth

In the fast-paced world we live in, it's easy to get caught up in the momentum of striving towards our goals without pausing to reflect on our progress. However, reflection and feedback are crucial components of personal and professional growth. They are the tools that allow us to assess where we are, adjust our course, and enhance our performance. In this chapter, we'll explore the power of reflection and feedback, and how to effectively integrate these practices into your journey toward success.

The Importance of Reflection

Reflection is the practice of looking back at your experiences, analyzing them, and drawing insights that can inform your future actions. It's about taking a step back from the hustle and bustle to consider how things are going, what's working, and what could be improved.

Why Reflect?

- **Self-Awareness:** Reflection helps you understand yourself better—your strengths, weaknesses, motivations, and patterns. This self-awareness is critical for personal growth and making informed decisions.
- **Learning from Experience:** By reflecting on past experiences, you can extract valuable lessons. What worked well? What didn't? What would you do differently next time? These insights are the building blocks of wisdom.
- **Course Correction:** Regular reflection allows you to adjust your goals and strategies. If you're off track,

reflection helps you identify the reasons and make necessary changes before it's too late.
- **Celebrating Success**: Reflection isn't just about finding faults; it's also about acknowledging and celebrating your successes. Celebrating your successes can increase your self-belief and drive.

How to Reflect Effectively

Schedule Regular Reflection Time: Make reflection a regular part of your routine. Whether it's daily, weekly, or monthly, set aside dedicated time to reflect on your experiences, progress, and emotions.
Ask the Right Questions: Effective reflection involves asking yourself probing questions. Some examples include:
   - What were my goals, and did I achieve them?
   - What difficulties did I experience, and how did I address them?
   - What valuable lessons did I take away?
   - Am I satisfied with my progress so far?
Use a Reflection Journal: Writing down your thoughts can help clarify them. Keep a journal where you document your reflections, insights, and lessons learned. Over time, this journal becomes a valuable resource that tracks your growth and evolution.
Be Honest with Yourself: Reflection is only useful if you're honest about your experiences. Acknowledge both your successes and areas for improvement without judgment. This honesty is crucial for genuine growth.
Incorporate Meditation or Mindfulness: Sometimes, reflection can be enhanced by practices like meditation or mindfulness, which help you focus on the present moment and gain deeper insights into your thoughts and feelings.

The Role of Feedback

Feedback is the external counterpart to reflection. While reflection is about self-assessment, feedback involves seeking input from others to gain a different perspective on your performance. Constructive feedback is one of the most powerful tools for growth, providing you with insights that you might not have considered on your own.

Why Seek Feedback?

- Identifying Blind Spots: We all have blind spots—areas where we're unaware of our shortcomings. Feedback helps identify these blind spots, allowing us to address them.
- Gaining New Perspectives: Feedback provides a fresh perspective on your work and behavior. Others may see things you don't, and their input can help you view your actions and decisions in a new light.
- Validating Your Approach: Positive feedback can validate that you're on the right track, reinforcing effective strategies and boosting your confidence.
- Encouraging Continuous Improvement: Feedback fosters a culture of continuous improvement. By regularly seeking input, you show a commitment to growth and excellence.

How to Seek and Use Feedback Effectively

Choose the Right People: Not all feedback is created equal. Seek feedback from people you trust, who have the knowledge and experience to provide constructive insights. This could be mentors, colleagues, supervisors, or even friends and family.
Be Specific in Your Request: When asking for feedback, be specific about the areas where you want input. For example, instead of asking, "How did I do?" you might ask, "What could I improve in my communication during meetings?"

Listen Actively: When receiving feedback, listen with an open mind. Avoid getting defensive or justifying your actions. Instead, focus on understanding the feedback and the perspective of the person providing it.

Ask Clarifying Questions: If feedback is unclear, don't hesitate to ask for clarification. This ensures that you fully understand the input and can apply it effectively.

Reflect on the Feedback: After receiving feedback, take time to reflect on it. How does it align with your self-assessment? What changes can you make based on the feedback? Integrate this reflection into your regular reflection practice.

Take Action: Feedback is only valuable if you act on it. Identify specific steps you can take to implement the feedback, and make these part of your action plan moving forward.

Express Gratitude: Providing feedback requires time and effort. Show appreciation to those who give you feedback, acknowledging their contribution to your growth.

The Synergy of Reflection and Feedback

While reflection and feedback are powerful on their own, they are even more effective when used together. Reflection allows you to assess your internal experience, while feedback provides external validation and new perspectives. Combined, they paint a comprehensive portrait of your progress and achievements.

Integrating Reflection and Feedback

Start with Reflection: Begin by reflecting on your performance and progress. Identify areas where you feel confident and areas where you could improve.

Seek Feedback: After reflecting, seek feedback on the same areas. Align your self-assessment with the feedback

you're getting. Are there any discrepancies? What new insights did the feedback provide?
Adjust and Implement: Based on your reflection and the feedback, adjust your goals, strategies, or behavior as needed. Create a plan for implementing the changes and track your progress over time.
Reflect Again: After implementing the changes, reflect again on the process. How did the feedback help? What did you learn from the experience? This cyclical process of reflection and feedback ensures continuous growth and improvement.

Creating a Culture of Reflection and Feedback

In addition to practicing reflection and feedback on a personal level, it's important to cultivate these practices in your work environment, whether you're leading a team or working within one. A culture that values reflection and feedback fosters growth, innovation, and collaboration.

How to Build This Culture

Lead by Example: Demonstrate the importance of reflection and feedback by practicing them yourself. Share your reflections with your team and actively seek their feedback.
Encourage Open Communication: Create an environment where team members feel comfortable sharing their thoughts, ideas, and feedback Create an environment that encourages candid and truthful communication without fear of criticism.
Offer Helpful Feedback: When providing feedback, aim to be constructive. Highlight strengths and areas for improvement, offering specific suggestions for growth.
Celebrate Learning: Recognize and celebrate the lessons learned from both successes and failures. This reinforces

the value of reflection and feedback as tools for continuous learning.
Incorporate Regular Check-Ins: Schedule regular check-ins with your team to discuss progress, reflect on recent experiences, and provide feedback. This ensures that reflection and feedback become an ongoing part of the work process.

Quick Wins

1. **Choose One Key Goal:** Identify one goal that you want to achieve in the next month. Write it down, and break it into three smaller milestones to make progress easier.
2. **Daily Intention Setting:** Each morning, set a specific intention for the day that aligns with your goal. It could be a small action, like researching a topic or making a phone call.
3. **Reflect on Past Successes:** Take 15 minutes to write down three past successes and analyze what made them possible. Use this insight to inform your current goal-setting process.
4. **Accountability Partner:** Reach out to a friend, family member, or colleague to act as your accountability partner. Share your goal with them and agree on regular check-ins.
5. **Visualize Success:** Spend five minutes each day visualizing yourself achieving your goal. Focus on how it will feel and the benefits it will bring.

Conclusion

Reflection and feedback are essential elements of personal and professional growth. They offer the understanding and viewpoints necessary to navigate life's challenges and achieve significant accomplishments. By integrating these practices into your routine, you create a powerful cycle of continuous improvement, ensuring that you're always moving forward with intention and clarity.

As you continue on your journey, remember that growth isn't just about setting goals and achieving them—it's about learning from the process, adapting to new information, and continually striving to become the best version of yourself. Through the power of reflection and feedback, you unlock the full potential of your efforts and set the stage for lasting success.

Worksheet for Chapter 3: Building a Personal Brand

A. Defining Your Brand

1. **What are the core values you want your personal brand to represent?**
   - Value 1: _____
   - Value 2: _____
   - Value 3: _____

2. **What skills or expertise do you want to be known for?**
   - Skill/Expertise 1: _____
   - Skill/Expertise 2: _____
   - Skill/Expertise 3: _____

3. **Who is your target audience? Who do you want to influence with your brand?**
   - _____
   - _____
   - _____

4. **What differentiates you from others in your field? Identify your unique selling proposition (USP):**
   - _____
   - _____
   - _____

B. Crafting Your Brand Story

1. Write a brief summary of your professional journey highlighting key achievements that align with your brand:
    - _____
    - _____
    - _____

2. Describe a challenge you overcame that shaped your professional identity:
    - _____
    - _____
    - _____

3. How does your personal story support the values and skills you want to be known for?
    - _____
    - _____
    - _____

C. Communicating Your Brand

1. List the platforms where you will promote your personal brand (e.g., LinkedIn, personal website, social media):
    - Platform 1:
    _____
    - Platform 2:
    _____
    - Platform 3:
    _____

2. **What type of content will you create to showcase your expertise and values?**
    - Content Type 1:
    _____
    _____

    - Content Type 2:
    _____
    _____

    - Content Type 3:
    _____
    _____

3. **Who in your network can help amplify your brand? How will you engage with them?**
    - Contact 1:
    _____
    _____

    - Contact 2:
    _____
    _____

    - Contact 3:
    _____
    _____

D. Planning with CLEAR Goals

1. **Collaborative:** Who can you collaborate with to enhance your personal brand?
    - _____
2. **Limited:** What specific actions will you take in the next month to strengthen your brand presence?

- Action 1:
  _____
  _____

- Action 2:
  _____
  _____

3. **Emotional:** Why is building your personal brand important to you? How does it align with your career aspirations?
   - _____
   - _____

4. **Appreciable:** What small wins can you achieve this week to advance your brand-building efforts?
   - Win 1:
     _____
     _____
   - Win 2:
     _____
     _____

5. **Refinable:** How will you adapt your brand strategy if you don't see the desired results?
   - _____
   - _____

E. Progress Tracking

1. **Monthly Review:** How have you progressed in building and promoting your personal brand this month?
   - _____
   - _____

2. **Adjustments:** What will you adjust in your strategy based on the feedback or outcomes you've received?

   - _____
   - _____

Chapter 4: The Balance of Ambition and Contentment

As we aim for success, we tend to concentrate on the motivation, hard work, and perseverance needed to achieve our objectives. But there is another side to this coin that is equally important—contentment. Understanding how to balance ambition with contentment is key to maintaining not only your motivation but also your well-being. In this chapter, we will explore how to cultivate this balance, ensuring that your pursuit of success is both fulfilling and sustainable.

Understanding Ambition and Contentment

Ambition and contentment might seem like opposites at first glance Ambition propels you toward your goals, while contentment helps you appreciate your current situation. Yet, these two qualities can coexist. When properly balanced, they can complement each other, creating a harmonious approach to personal and professional growth.

Ambition: The Drive to Achieve

Ambition is the fuel that propels you toward your dreams. It's what keeps you striving for more, pushing past obstacles, and continuously improving yourself. Ambition is essential for growth because it challenges you to step out of your comfort zone and aim for higher levels of success.

The Power of Ambition

Motivation: Ambition keeps you motivated, giving you the energy and focus to pursue your goals with determination.

Resilience: When faced with setbacks, your ambition helps you persevere, viewing challenges as opportunities to learn and grow.
Vision: Ambition gives you a sense of direction, helping you to set clear goals and map out a path to achieve them.
Innovation: Ambition drives creativity and innovation, pushing you to think outside the box and explore new possibilities.

Contentment: The Art of Satisfaction

Contentment, on the other hand, is the ability to find peace and satisfaction in the present moment. It's about appreciating what you have, recognizing your achievements, and being at ease with where you are in life. Contentment provides the emotional stability that allows you to pursue your goals without being consumed by them.

The Power of Contentment

Inner Peace: Contentment brings a sense of calm and peace, reducing stress and anxiety by allowing you to accept things as they are.
Gratitude: Being content encourages gratitude, helping you to appreciate the positives in your life, even as you work towards new goals.
Satisfaction: Contentment allows you to feel satisfied with your progress, preventing burnout by giving you time to rest and recharge.
Balanced Perspective: Contentment helps you maintain a balanced perspective, reminding you that success is not just about achieving external goals but also about finding happiness and fulfillment in the journey.
The Dangers of Imbalance
When ambition and contentment are out of balance, it can lead to a variety of problems. Too much ambition without

contentment can result in chronic dissatisfaction, stress, and burnout. On the other hand, too much contentment without ambition can lead to complacency, stagnation, and a lack of progress.

The Risks of Over-Ambition

Burnout: Constantly pushing yourself without taking time to rest can lead to burnout, characterized by exhaustion, stress, and a loss of motivation.
Discontent: Over-ambition can lead to a perpetual state of discontent, where you're never satisfied with your achievements and always striving for more.
Neglect of Well-being: Focusing solely on ambition can cause you to neglect other important aspects of your life, such as health, relationships, and mental well-being.
Tunnel Vision: Over-ambition can narrow your focus, causing you to miss out on the joy and fulfillment that comes from the journey itself.

The Risks of Over-Contentment

Complacency: Without ambition, you may become complacent, settling for less than what you're capable of achieving.
Lack of Growth: Over-contentment can lead to a lack of personal and professional growth, as you may stop challenging yourself to improve.
Missed Opportunities: Being too content can cause you to miss out on opportunities for advancement, innovation, and success.
Stagnation: Without ambition, you may find yourself stuck in a rut, with little motivation to pursue new goals or explore new possibilities.

Strategies for Balancing Ambition and Contentment

Finding the right balance between ambition and contentment is a dynamic process. It requires self-awareness, reflection, and a commitment to maintaining both your drive for success and your ability to appreciate the present moment.

1. Set Meaningful Goals

One of the keys to balancing ambition and contentment is to set meaningful goals. These are goals that align with your values, passions, and long-term vision for your life. When your goals are meaningful, they inspire ambition while also fostering a sense of purpose and fulfillment.

> **Align with Your Values:** Ensure that your goals reflect your core values and beliefs. This alignment creates a sense of authenticity and satisfaction in your pursuit of success.
> **Focus on Long-Term Fulfillment:** Choose goals that contribute to your long-term happiness and well-being, rather than just short-term gains.
> **Incorporate Balance:** Include goals that promote balance in your life, such as goals related to health, relationships, and personal growth.

2. Practice Gratitude

Gratitude is a powerful antidote to over-ambition. By regularly practicing gratitude, you can cultivate contentment while still maintaining your drive for success.

> **Daily Gratitude Practice:** Take a few minutes each day to reflect on what you're grateful for. This

could include your achievements, the support of loved ones, or simple pleasures in life.
Celebrate Milestones: Acknowledge and celebrate your progress, even the smallest steps. This reinforces contentment and keeps you motivated.
Gratitude Journal: Keep a gratitude journal where you document the things you're thankful for. Reviewing this journal regularly can help maintain a balanced perspective.

3. Schedule Downtime

To prevent burnout and maintain contentment, it's important to schedule regular downtime. This is time dedicated to rest, relaxation, and activities that bring you joy and fulfillment outside of your work or goals.

Invest in Yourself: Make self-care a priority. This includes taking care of your physical, mental, and emotional health.
Engage in Hobbies: Spend time on hobbies or activities that you enjoy purely for the pleasure they bring, without any pressure to achieve.
Unplug Regularly: Take breaks from work and technology to recharge your mind and body. This could be through nature walks, meditation, or spending time with loved ones.

4. Reflect and Adjust

Regular reflection allows you to assess whether your ambition and contentment are in balance. It gives you the opportunity to make adjustments as needed to maintain a healthy and sustainable approach to your goals.

Regular Check-Ins: Schedule regular check-ins with yourself to reflect on your progress, well-

being, and overall satisfaction. Are you feeling motivated and content, or is there an imbalance?
Adjust Your Goals: If you notice signs of over-ambition or over-contentment, adjust your goals and strategies accordingly. This might involve scaling back on certain ambitions or setting new challenges.
Seek Feedback: Feedback from trusted friends, mentors, or colleagues can provide valuable insights into how well you're balancing ambition and contentment. Use this feedback to inform your reflection and adjustments.

5. Cultivate a Growth Mindset

A growth mindset is the belief that you can develop your abilities and achieve success through effort, learning, and persistence. This mindset encourages you to embrace challenges and view failures as opportunities for growth, which can help you balance ambition with contentment.

Embrace Challenges: View challenges as opportunities to learn and grow, rather than as threats to your success. This mindset fosters resilience and a healthy drive for achievement.
Learn from Setbacks: When you encounter setbacks, reflect on what you can learn from the experience. This helps you maintain contentment by focusing on growth rather than perfection.
Celebrate Effort: Recognize and celebrate the effort you put into your goals, regardless of the outcome. This reinforces contentment and motivates continued progress.

Quick Wins

1. **Gratitude Practice**: Start a daily gratitude journal where you write down three things you're grateful for each day. This will help cultivate contentment while pursuing your goals.
2. **Take a Relaxation Break**: Schedule a 10-minute break today to do something relaxing, like taking a walk, meditating, or listening to your favorite music. This will help balance your ambition with contentment.
3. **Celebrate a Small Win**: Reflect on something you've accomplished recently, no matter how small. Take a moment to celebrate it and appreciate your progress.
4. **Reflect on Work-Life Balance**: Spend 15 minutes assessing your current work-life balance. Identify one area where you can make a small adjustment to improve your well-being.
5. **Plan a Downtime Activity**: Schedule an activity this week that is purely for relaxation or enjoyment, such as reading a book, spending time with loved ones, or pursuing a hobby.

Conclusion

Balancing ambition with contentment is essential for achieving success in a way that is both fulfilling and sustainable. By setting meaningful goals, practicing gratitude, scheduling downtime, reflecting regularly, and cultivating a growth mindset, you can maintain the drive to achieve your dreams while also finding peace and satisfaction in the present moment.

Remember that true success is not just about reaching the finish line—it's about enjoying the journey along the way. By embracing both ambition and contentment, you create a balanced approach to life that nurtures both your aspirations and your well-being.

Worksheet for Chapter 4: Overcoming Setbacks with Integrity and Resilience

A. Identifying Setbacks

1. What recent setback or challenge have you faced in your career?
    - _____
    - _____

2. What were the initial thoughts or emotions you experienced?
    - _____
    - _____

3. What impact did this setback have on your work and mindset?
    - _____
    - _____

B. Analyzing the Situation

1. What factors contributed to this setback? Consider both internal and external factors.
    - Internal Factor 1:
      _____
      _____

    - Internal Factor 2:
      _____
      _____

    - External Factor 1:
      _____
      _____

- External Factor 2:
  _____
  _____

2. What could you have done differently to potentially avoid or lessen the setback?
   - _____
   - _____

3. How did you respond to the setback initially? Was your response aligned with your values?
   - _____
   - _____

C. Developing Resilience

1. What coping strategies did you use, and how effective were they?
   - Strategy 1:
     _____
     _____
   - Strategy 2:
     _____
     _____
   - Effectiveness:
     _____
     _____

2. What lessons did you learn from this setback that can help you in the future?
   - Lesson 1:
     _____
     _____

- Lesson 2:
  _____
  _____

3. **How can you reframe this setback as an opportunity for growth?**
   - _____
   - _____

D. Integrity in Action

1. **In what ways did you maintain your integrity while dealing with this setback?**
   - _____
   - _____

2. **How can you ensure that your actions align with your core values even in challenging situations?**
   - _____
   - _____

3. **What steps will you take to rebuild trust and credibility if they were affected?**
   - _____
   - _____

E. Planning with CLEAR Goals

1. **Collaborative:** Who can you reach out to for support or advice in overcoming similar challenges in the future?
   - _____
   - _____

2. **Limited:** What specific actions can you take to prevent this setback from recurring?
    - Action 1:
      _____
      _____
    - Action 2:
      _____
      _____

3. **Emotional:** How will overcoming this setback contribute to your long-term success?
    - _____
    - _____

4. **Appreciable:** What small steps can you take now to start recovering from the setback?
    - Step 1:
      _____
      _____
    - Step 2:
      _____
      _____

5. **Refinable:** How will you adapt your approach if your initial recovery efforts don't go as planned?
    - _____
    - _____

F. Progress Tracking

1. **Monthly Review:** What progress have you made in overcoming the setback and moving forward?
    - _____
    - _____

2. **Adjustments:** What further adjustments or strategies will you implement to ensure continuous improvement?

    o _____
    o _____

Chapter 5: Staying Motivated – Managing Stress and Building Resilience

Introduction: The Challenge of Sustained Motivation

In the fast-paced world we live in, staying motivated can be a significant challenge, especially when faced with stress, setbacks, or the sheer monotony of routine. This chapter is dedicated to helping you maintain your drive, manage stress effectively, and build resilience so you can sustain long-term motivation. By integrating practical strategies, emotional regulation techniques, and real-life examples, you'll be equipped to keep your momentum going even when the going gets tough.

Understanding the Role of Motivation in Success

Motivation is the fuel that powers your journey towards achieving your goals. It's what gets you started, keeps you going, and helps you overcome obstacles. However, motivation isn't always a constant force. It can ebb and flow, influenced by external factors like stress, workload, and personal challenges.

Comprehending the psychology of motivation can be a game-changer. Motivation can be intrinsic (driven by internal desires like personal growth) or extrinsic (fueled by external rewards like recognition or money). Both types are important, but finding the right balance is key to maintaining long-term motivation. For example, while a promotion at work might provide an extrinsic push, your intrinsic desire to excel in your field will sustain you over the long haul.

Managing Stress: The Silent Motivation Killer

Stress is often the silent killer of motivation. When left unchecked, it can lead to burnout, reduced productivity, and a loss of enthusiasm. To maintain motivation, it's essential to develop effective stress management techniques.

One approach is to view stress through the lens of the "stress curve," which suggests that a moderate level of stress can actually enhance performance. **This is called eustress, or positive stress.** However, when stress becomes too high, it turns into distress, leading to negative outcomes like anxiety and burnout.

Stress Management Techniques:
Mindfulness Meditation: Regular mindfulness practice can help you stay centered and reduce stress by focusing on the present moment.
Breathing Exercises: Simple breathing techniques, like the 4-7-8 method, can instantly calm your nervous system and reduce stress levels.
Stay Active: Regular physical activity is a proven stress buster. It releases endorphins, the body's natural stress-fighting chemicals, which help you feel more relaxed and motivated.

Building Resilience: The Foundation of Sustained Motivation

Resilience is the capacity to recover from setbacks, and it's essential for long-lasting motivation. Life is unpredictable, and setbacks are inevitable. However, your response to these challenges determines your long-term success.

Strategies for Building Resilience:

Growth Mindset: Adopt a growth mindset, which is the belief that you can develop your abilities through effort and learning. This mindset helps you see challenges as stepping stones to growth, instead of road blocks.
Positive Reframing: Train yourself to reframe negative situations in a more positive light. For example, instead of perceiving a setback as a failure, see it as a chance to grow.
Support Networks: Surround yourself with a strong support network of friends, family, and colleagues. Having people to lean on during tough times can significantly boost your resilience.

Emotional Regulation: Keeping Your Emotions in Check

Emotional regulation is the skill of controlling and responding to your feelings in a positive and constructive manner. It's crucial for maintaining motivation, especially when faced with stress or setbacks.

Emotional Regulation Techniques:

Cognitive Restructuring: This technique involves changing the way you think about a situation to alter your emotional response. For example, if you're feeling overwhelmed by a task, break it down into smaller, more manageable steps to reduce anxiety.
Journaling: Writing about your thoughts and feelings can help you process emotions and gain clarity. It's also a great way to track your progress and stay motivated.
Visualization: Visualize yourself successfully completing a challenging task. This can boost your confidence and motivation, making the task feel less daunting.

Real-Life Examples: Stories of Resilience and Motivation

Example 1: Sarah's Journey to Overcoming Burnout

Sarah was a high-achieving marketing manager who loved her job. But after years of giving it her all, she started to feel the creeping signs of burnout—exhaustion, cynicism, and a lack of accomplishment. It reached a point where she dreaded going to work every day. Realizing something needed to change, Sarah sought help. She started practicing mindfulness and journaling daily, which helped her reconnect with her purpose and manage her stress levels. She also set boundaries, learned to delegate tasks, and took time off to recharge. Over time, Sarah regained her enthusiasm for her work and found a sustainable balance between her career and personal life.

Example 2: Mark's Path to Building Resilience

Mark, a successful freelance graphic designer, faced a significant challenge when his biggest client decided to take their business in-house, leaving him with a substantial gap in his income. Initially, this setback shook his confidence, but Mark chose to view it as an opportunity to diversify his client base. He took this time to refine his portfolio, reach out to new potential clients, and invest in learning new skills that broadened his service offerings. Despite the initial loss, Mark's resilience allowed him to rebuild stronger than before, eventually landing contracts with two major clients in entirely new industries.

Example 3: Lila's Emotional Regulation Strategy

Lila was an entrepreneur with big dreams, but the emotional highs and lows of starting her own business often left her feeling overwhelmed. After nearly quitting several times, Lila decided to invest in her mental well-being. She began working with a coach who introduced her to cognitive restructuring techniques. Whenever Lila encountered a setback, she would pause, journal her thoughts, and then challenge her negative assumptions by asking herself questions like, "What can I learn from this?" and "How can this make me stronger?" This approach helped Lila maintain her motivation and continue growing her business despite the inevitable challenges of entrepreneurship.

Maintaining Motivation in the Long-Term
Long-term motivation requires ongoing effort and self-awareness. Here are some tips to keep your enthusiasm going.
Regularly Revisit Your Goals: Periodically review and adjust your goals to ensure they remain relevant and aligned with your values and aspirations.
Celebrate Small Wins: Every step forward is a victory. Celebrate them to stay inspired
Stay Connected to Your "Why": Continuously remind yourself of the reasons behind your goals. Connecting your actions to a deeper purpose can fuel your motivation even during challenging times.

Quick Wins:

1. **Practice 5-Minute Breathing Exercises**: Take five minutes out of your day to practice deep breathing or a quick mindfulness exercise. This simple practice can reduce stress and help you stay focused.
2. **Set a Small, Achievable Goal for the Week**: Identify one specific, manageable goal that you can accomplish this week. Achieving it will give you a

quick confidence boost and keep your motivation high.
3. **Schedule a Resilience-Boosting Activity**: Plan an activity that helps you build resilience, such as spending time with loved ones, engaging in a hobby, or taking a short course to develop a new skill.
4. **Create a "Positive Reframe" Journal**: Start a journal where you write down challenges you face and then reframe them in a more positive light. This practice will help you build a more resilient mindset.
5. **Visualize a Successful Outcome**: Spend a few minutes each day visualizing the successful completion of a goal. Imagine how it feels and the benefits it brings, which can help keep you motivated.

Conclusion

Sustaining motivation over the long term is not just about initial enthusiasm or setting the right goals; it's about cultivating resilience, managing stress, and finding personal meaning in your journey. The strategies outlined in this chapter are designed to equip you with the tools necessary to navigate the inevitable ups and downs that accompany any significant endeavor. By practicing emotional regulation, building resilience, and maintaining a deep connection to your "why," you can continue to move forward even when motivation wanes.

Remember, motivation isn't about always feeling excited or driven. It's about having the resilience to continue moving forward, even when faced with obstacles or setbacks. By integrating the practices of stress management, emotional regulation, and resilience-building into your daily life, you create a foundation for sustained motivation that can weather the challenges ahead.

As you continue your journey, keep in mind that every setback is an opportunity for growth, every stressor can be managed, and every dip in motivation can be reversed. The key is to stay focused, keep your eyes on the prize, and remember that each step you take brings you closer to your goals.

Worksheet for Chapter 5: Building and Leveraging a Powerful Network

A. Assessing Your Current Network

1. List key individuals in your current professional network.
   - _____
   - _____

2. How do these connections currently support your career goals?
   - _____
   - _____

3. Which areas of your network need strengthening? Consider areas where you lack connections or where your current connections are not as effective.
   - _____
   - _____

B. Identifying Networking Opportunities

1. What industry events, conferences, or online communities could you participate in to expand your network?
   - Event 1: _____
     _____
   - Event 2: _____
     _____

AMEERAYY ALI

2. Which professionals or organizations would be valuable additions to your network?
    - Professional 1: _____
    - Organization 1: _____

3. How can you position yourself to connect with these individuals or groups?
    - _____
    - _____

C. Enhancing Your Networking Skills

1. Rate your current networking skills (e.g., communication, follow-up, relationship-building) on a scale of 1-10.
    - Communication: _____
    - Follow-Up: _____
    - Relationship-Building: _____

2. What areas of networking do you need to improve, and how will you do it?
    - Area 1: _____
    - Improvement Strategy: _____
    - Area 2: _____

AMEERAYY ALI

- Improvement Strategy:
  _____
  _____

3. **How will you create value for others in your network? Consider what skills, knowledge, or resources you can offer.**
   - _____
   - _____

D. Maintaining and Growing Relationships

1. **How often do you check in with key contacts in your network? List any contacts you haven't engaged with recently and plan how to reconnect.**
   - Contact 1:
     _____
   - Reconnection Plan:
     _____
   - Contact 2:
     _____
   - Reconnection Plan:
     _____

2. **How will you continue to nurture these relationships over time?**
   - _____
   - _____

3. What methods (e.g., social media, emails, in-person meetings) will you use to stay in touch and keep your network active?
   - _____
   - _____

E. Strategic Networking with CLEAR Goals

1. **Collaborative:** Who in your network can you collaborate with on a project or idea?
   - _____
   - _____
2. **Limited:** What specific networking activities will you focus on in the next month?
   - Activity 1:

   _____

   _____

   - Activity 2:

   _____

   _____

3. **Emotional:** How does building and maintaining a strong network make you feel about your career trajectory?
   - _____
   - _____
4. **Appreciable:** What small steps can you take today to expand your network?
   - Step 1:

   _____

   _____

- Step 2: _____
  _____

5. **Refinable:** How will you adjust your networking strategy if it's not yielding the desired results?
   - _____
   - _____

F. Progress Tracking

1. **Monthly Review:** How many new meaningful connections have you made this month?
   - _____
   - _____

2. **Adjustments:** What further networking strategies will you implement to achieve your goals?
   - _____
   - _____

Chapter 6: Navigating Career Transitions – Planning Your Next Move

Navigating Career Transitions

Career transitions are inevitable. Whether it's a promotion, a lateral move within your current company, a complete career change, or even stepping back for personal reasons, the key to managing these transitions is preparation and strategic planning. This chapter is designed to help you understand the dynamics of career transitions, create a strategic plan, and execute it successfully while leveraging digital tools and resources.

Understanding Career Transitions

While career transitions offer new opportunities, they can also be a source of anxiety and doubt. Understanding the different types of career transitions and recognizing when they are necessary can help you make informed decisions. Some common types of career transitions include:

- **Promotions**: Moving up the ladder within your current organization.
- **Lateral Moves**: Shifting to a different role or department at the same level.
- **Career Change**: Switching to a new industry or profession entirely.
- **Relocation**: Moving to a new geographic location for work.
- **Entrepreneurship**: Venturing into the world of entrepreneurship.
- **Re-entry**: Rejoining the workforce after a career break.

Each of these transitions presents its own set of challenges and opportunities. By understanding the type of transition you're facing, you can better prepare for it.

Career Transition Checklist
To ensure a smooth career transition, it's essential to have a clear action plan. **Start with a self-assessment:** evaluate your current job satisfaction, identify your career goals, and determine your strengths, skills, and areas for development. Consider your values and career goals.

Then, move on to research and exploration. **Investigate potential career paths**, industries, or roles that interest you, and network with professionals in your desired field to gain insights. Consider informational interviews or job shadowing to understand the day-to-day realities of different roles.

Conduct a skills gap analysis to identify any skills or qualifications you need to acquire for your desired transition.

Enroll in relevant courses, certifications, or training programs, and seek opportunities to gain experience, such as volunteering or freelancing.

Create an Action Plan and set specific, achievable goals for your career transition, such as completing a course, attending networking events, or applying for a certain number of jobs.

Financial planning is also crucial; assess your financial situation, **create a budget for the transition period**, and consider the potential impact on your income and lifestyle. It's wise to build an emergency fund to cushion any financial instability.

Building connections and showcasing your skills online are essential. Make sure your resume, LinkedIn, and other professional profiles are up-to-date. Reach out to your network for advice, referrals, and job leads, and attend industry events, workshops, and conferences to expand your network.

When it comes to application and interview preparation, **tailor your resume and cover letter** to each role or industry, and practice common interview questions while refining your pitch. Research the company culture and align your responses with their values.

As you approach decision-making, **weigh the pros and cons of each opportunity,** considering how each option aligns with your long-term career goals and personal life. Listen to your instincts and make a choice that feels authentic.

Once you've secured a new role or position, **focus on onboarding and integration** by building relationships with your new colleagues, seeking feedback early and often, and being patient with yourself as you adapt to new challenges and environments.

Strategic Planning for Transitions

Planning for a career transition requires a strategic approach. Here's a step-by-step guide to creating a comprehensive plan.

Set Clear Objectives: Define what you want to achieve with this transition. Is it a higher salary, more job satisfaction, or a better work-life balance?

- **Identify Key Resources**: Determine the resources you'll need, such as education, networking, or financial savings.
- **Create a Timeline**: Set realistic deadlines for each stage of your transition. Divide the process into smaller parts
- **Monitor Progress**: Regularly review your plan to ensure you're on track. Adjust your strategy as needed based on new information or changing circumstances.
- **Seek Support**: A career coach or mentor can offer valuable advice and help you stay on track."
- **Prepare for Challenges**: Anticipate potential obstacles and develop contingency plans. Whether it's a job offer falling through or unexpected personal commitments, being prepared can help you stay resilient.

Digital Tools for Transition

In today's digital age, several tools can aid in your career transition:

- **LinkedIn**: Use LinkedIn to network, find job opportunities, and showcase your skills and accomplishments. Engage with industry-specific groups and follow companies you're interested in.
- **Glassdoor**: Research potential employers, read reviews, and get insights into company cultures and salary expectations.
- **Indeed**: Use job search engines like Indeed to explore opportunities in your desired field.
- **Skillshare/Udemy/Coursera**: These platforms offer a wide range of online courses to help you acquire new skills or enhance existing ones.
- **Trello/Asana**: Project management tools like Trello or Asana can help you organize your

AMEERAYY ALI

transition plan, set deadlines, and track your progress.

Real-Life Examples: Stories of Successful Transitions.

Example 1: Emma's Shift from Corporate to Non-Profit Sector

Emma had spent over a decade climbing the corporate ladder in the financial services industry. While she was successful, she felt unfulfilled and yearned to make a difference in the world. After careful self-assessment and research, she decided to transition into the non-profit sector, focusing on financial literacy programs for underprivileged communities. Emma used her skills in financial management to bring a unique perspective to the non-profit world. She started volunteering part-time while still in her corporate job, eventually landing a full-time role with a non-profit organization. The transition was challenging, but Emma's strategic planning, networking, and skills development paid off, and she found renewed purpose in her work.

Example 2: Jason's Career Change to Tech after a Layoff

Jason was a middle manager in a manufacturing company when he was laid off due to downsizing. Rather than seeing this as a setback, Jason viewed it as an opportunity to pursue his passion for technology. He enrolled in an online coding boot camp, leveraged his existing network to connect with tech professionals, and took on freelance projects to build his portfolio. Within a year, Jason successfully transitioned into a new role as a software developer. His story shows the value of resilience, learning, and networking.

Example 3: Laura's Lateral Move for Work-Life Balance

Laura was a marketing director at a fast-paced advertising agency, but the demands of the job were taking a toll on her personal life. She wanted more balance and decided to make a lateral move to an in-house marketing position with a company that valued work-life balance. Laura updated her resume to highlight her relevant skills, researched companies with strong work-life balance cultures, and networked with contacts in her target industry. The transition allowed Laura to maintain her professional level while achieving the personal balance she sought.

Quick Wins

- **Update Your LinkedIn Profile**: A fresh LinkedIn profile that reflects your current career goals and skills is an immediate step you can take to increase your visibility to potential employers or connections.
- **Attend an Industry Event**: Find an upcoming conference, webinar, or networking event related to your desired career path. Engaging with industry professionals can provide valuable insights and open doors to new opportunities.
- **Enroll in a Relevant Course**: Identify one skill that is critical for your next career move and enroll in a short online course to build that skill.
- **Reach Out to a Mentor**: Contact a mentor or industry expert for advice on navigating your career transition. Their experience can provide valuable perspective and guidance.
- **Create a Transition Budget**: Outline your finances and create a budget that accounts for any potential income gaps or additional expenses

during your transition. This quick win ensures financial stability as you navigate your career move.

Conclusion

Navigating a career transition can be both exhilarating and challenging. The key to success lies in meticulous preparation and a well-thought-out strategy. By understanding the nuances of different types of career transitions and following a structured approach, you can manage this process effectively. Embrace the opportunity to reassess your goals, acquire new skills, and adapt to new environments. Each transition is a chance for growth and a step toward achieving a more fulfilling professional life.

Every transition is an opportunity for growth. They offer valuable opportunities to realign your career path with your evolving goals and aspirations. Stay focused on your objectives, leverage available resources, and maintain a positive mindset as you navigate these changes. With resilience and strategic planning, you can turn these transitions into significant milestones on your journey to career success.

Worksheet for Chapter 6: Navigating Career Transitions – Planning Your Next Move

A. Evaluating Your Current Position

1. What do you enjoy most about your current role?
    - _____
    - _____

2. What challenges or dissatisfactions are you experiencing?
    - _____
    - _____

3. What are your reasons for considering a career transition?
    - _____
    - _____

B. Defining Your Career Transition Goals

1. What are your top priorities for your next career move?
    - Priority 1:
      _____
      _____
    - Priority 2:
      _____
      _____

2. Which skills, experiences, or qualifications do you want to develop further?
    - _____
    - _____

AMEERAYY ALI

3. **What industries or roles are you interested in exploring?**
    - Industry/Role 1:
      _____
      _____
    - Industry/Role 2:
      _____
      _____

C. Researching Potential Opportunities

1. **List any companies, organizations, or sectors that align with your career goals.**
    - Company/Organization 1:
      _____
      _____
    - Sector 1:
      _____
      _____

2. **How does the job market look in these areas? What trends or demands should you be aware of?**
    - _____
    - _____

3. **Who can you reach out to in your network for advice or insights into these opportunities?**
    - Contact 1:
      _____
      _____
    - Contact 2:
      _____
      _____

D. Developing a Transition Plan

1. **What steps will you take to prepare for this transition (e.g., additional training, certifications, networking)?**
    - Step 1:

    _____

    _____

    - Step 2:

    _____

    _____

2. **What is your timeline for making this career move?**
    - _____
    - _____

3. **How will you manage the financial and personal impacts of this transition?**
    - _____
    - _____

E. Creating CLEAR Career Transition Goals

1. **Collaborative:** Who will you involve in your career transition planning for support and advice?
    - _____
2. **Limited:** What specific, manageable tasks will you focus on in the next 30 days to progress your transition?
    - Task 1:

    _____

    _____

- Task 2:
    _____
    _____

3. **Emotional:** How does this transition align with your values and long-term aspirations?
    - _____

4. **Appreciable:** What small milestones will mark your progress during this transition?
    - Milestone 1:
    _____
    _____
    - Milestone 2:
    _____
    _____

5. **Refinable:** How will you adjust your plan if you encounter unexpected challenges?
    - _____
    - _____

F. Tracking Your Progress

1. **Monthly Review:** What progress have you made toward your career transition this month?
    - _____
    - _____

2. **Next Steps:** What further actions will you take to move closer to your career goals?
    - _____
    - _____

Chapter 7: Navigating Office Politics and Digital Dynamics

Introduction: The Double-Edged Sword of Office Politics and Digital Dynamics

In today's interconnected world, your workplace isn't just the physical office but also extends into the digital realm. Navigating office politics and managing digital dynamics have become essential skills for anyone seeking to advance in their career. While these aspects of professional life can be challenging, understanding their intricacies and mastering them can significantly boost your career trajectory.

Understanding Office Politics: The Unspoken Rules

Office politics often carry a negative connotation, but when navigated correctly, they can work in your favor. The key is to understand the unspoken rules of your workplace and use them strategically without compromising your integrity.

- **The Landscape of Office Politics:** Office politics refers to the power dynamics, alliances, and relationships that influence decisions and opportunities in the workplace. Recognizing the key players and understanding their motivations is crucial.
- **The Role of Influence and Perception:** How you are perceived by others in your organization can significantly impact your career. Developing a positive reputation, building alliances, and influencing decisions require careful and deliberate actions.

- **Common Political Scenarios:** Explore common office scenarios, such as dealing with difficult colleagues, navigating power struggles, and managing conflicts of interest. Understanding these scenarios allows you to anticipate challenges and respond effectively.

Strategic Tips for Navigating Office Politics

- **Build Authentic Relationships:** Establishing genuine connections with colleagues across all levels of the organization can create a strong support network. Be consistent, trustworthy, and respectful in your interactions.
- **Stay Neutral but Informed:** Avoid taking sides in workplace conflicts. Instead, remain neutral, gather information, and make informed decisions that align with your professional goals and values.
- **Communicate Transparently:** Keep it real! Honesty builds trust. When dealing with sensitive issues, ensure your messaging is clear, concise, and empathetic.
- **Practice Active Listening:** Pay close attention to what is said and, equally important, to what is not said. Active listening helps you pick up on underlying tensions or opportunities that may not be immediately obvious.

Impact of Digital Dynamics: Your Online Presence Matters

In today's digital world, how you present yourself online reflects your professional brand. Social media and digital communication tools have amplified the reach and impact of office politics, making it essential to manage your digital footprint carefully.

- **The Power of Social Media:** Platforms like LinkedIn, Twitter, and even Facebook can significantly impact your career. How you present yourself online can influence colleagues, clients, and future employers.
- **Digital Communication Nuances:** Emails, instant messaging, and video calls are part of everyday communication. Understanding the nuances of these mediums—such as tone, timing, and audience—can help you navigate potential pitfalls.
- **Managing Your Digital Reputation:** Just as in the physical workplace, your actions online have consequences. Regularly audit your social media profiles, remove any content that may be viewed negatively, and be mindful of what you post or share.

Maintaining an Effective Online Presence

- **Personal Branding:** Develop a strong, consistent personal brand across all digital platforms. Highlight your strengths, showcase your achievements, and align your online presence with your career goals.
- **Engage Thoughtfully:** Participate in online discussions, share relevant content, and engage with others in your industry. Thoughtful engagement can position you as a knowledgeable and approachable professional.
- **Protect Your Privacy:** Keep your secrets safe! Be cautious about sharing personal info online. Adjust privacy settings to control who sees your content and be mindful of the boundaries between your personal and professional life.

Real-World Scenarios: Case Studies of Successful Navigation

Case Study 1: Leveraging Office Politics for a Promotion

Eila, a mid-level manager at a tech company, strategically positioned herself for a promotion by building strong relationships with key decision-makers. She identified and aligned with influential allies, such as the VP of Sales and the Director of Operations, who could champion her cause. By consistently delivering exceptional results and proactively sharing her accomplishments, Sarah demonstrated her value and successfully secured a senior management role.

Case Study 2: Managing a Digital Crisis

Rohan, a social media manager, faced a backlash after a tweet about a controversial topic was misinterpreted. He responded swiftly by issuing a public apology and clarifying his stance through a follow-up post. Additionally, he engaged in open dialogue with critics to address their concerns and provided context for his original tweet. This transparent approach helped James restore his reputation and rebuild trust within his professional community.

Quick Wins:

- **Conduct a Social Media Audit:** Set aside 30 minutes to go through your social media profiles. Remove any content that could be perceived as unprofessional or misaligned with your career goals.
- **Strengthen Key Connections:** Identify three influential people in your organization or industry. Reach out to schedule a coffee meeting, lunch, or a

virtual catch-up to foster stronger professional relationships.
- **Polish Your Online Presence:** Update your LinkedIn profile or professional bio to accurately reflect your current skills, achievements, and aspirations. Make sure your online presence clearly showcases the skills and experience you offer.
- **Enhance Digital Communication:** For the next week, be mindful of your tone and clarity in all digital communications. Aim to be concise, professional, and empathetic, ensuring your messages are received as intended.
- **Observe Office Dynamics:** Spend the next few days observing the interactions and power dynamics within your workplace. Take note of who influences decisions, and consider how you can align your actions with your career objectives.

Conclusion:

Handling office relationships and digital interactions requires a careful blend of assertiveness and ethical behavior. By understanding the underlying power dynamics and building authentic relationships within your workplace, you can leverage these insights to your advantage. Effective communication, strategic influence, and maintaining a neutral stance during conflicts are essential skills that can help you thrive in complex professional environments. Additionally, managing your digital presence with the same level of care ensures that your online interactions align with your professional goals, enhancing your reputation and opportunities.

Embracing these strategies will empower you to turn potential challenges into opportunities for growth. Whether it's through building strong networks, refining your personal brand, or practicing thoughtful digital engagement, these practices will support your journey toward career success. As you apply these principles, remember that both your physical and digital interactions shape your professional trajectory. By staying proactive and adaptable, you can navigate the intricate landscape of office politics and digital dynamics with confidence and poise.

Worksheet for Chapter 7: Building and Leveraging Your Professional Network

A. Assessing Your Current Network

1. Who are the key individuals currently in your professional network?
    - _____
    - _____

2. How have these connections supported your career so far?
    - _____
    - _____

3. Are there any gaps in your network (e.g., industries, roles, expertise)?
    - _____
    - _____

B. Expanding Your Network

1. Identify three new connections you'd like to make.
    - Connection 1:
      _____
      _____
    - Connection 2:
      _____
      _____
    - Connection 3:
      _____
      _____

2. What strategies will you use to approach these individuals (e.g., LinkedIn, networking events, and referrals)?
   - Strategy 1:
     _____
     _____
   - Strategy 2:
     _____
     _____

3. Which professional groups, associations, or communities can you join to expand your network?
   - Group/Association 1:
     _____
     _____
   - Group/Association 2:
     _____
     _____

C. Strengthening Existing Relationships

1. How can you provide value to your current connections (e.g., sharing resources, offering support)?
   - _____
   - _____

2. Who in your network can you reach out to this week to strengthen your relationship?
   - Contact 1:
     _____
     _____

- Contact 2: _____
_____

3. What actions will you take to maintain consistent communication with your network?
   - _____
   - _____

D. Leveraging Your Network for Career Growth

1. Which connections can help you achieve your current career goals?
   - _____
   - _____

2. How can you effectively communicate your career goals to your network?
   - _____
   - _____

3. What opportunities (e.g., job openings, projects, collaborations) can your network help you discover?
   - Opportunity 1: _____
   _____
   - Opportunity 2: _____
   _____

E. Creating CLEAR Networking Goals

1. **Collaborative:** How will you collaborate with your network to achieve mutual goals?
   - _____

2. **Limited:** What specific networking activities will you focus on this month?
    - Activity 1:
      _____
    - Activity 2:
      _____

3. **Emotional:** How does networking align with your personal values and career aspirations?
    - _____

4. **Appreciable:** What milestones will indicate that your networking efforts are paying off?
    - Milestone 1:
      _____
    - Milestone 2:
      _____

5. **Refinable:** How will you adjust your networking strategy if certain connections don't pan out?
    - _____
    - _____

F. Tracking Your Progress

1. **Monthly Review:** How has your network grown or strengthened this month?
    - _____
    - _____

2. **Next Steps:** What will you do next to leverage your network more effectively?

   o _____
   o _____

Chapter 8: Never stop learning! Stay ahead of the game.

The Imperative of Lifelong Learning: Adapting to Change

In today's rapidly evolving job market, continuous learning isn't just an advantage—it's a necessity. The pace of technological advancement, industry shifts, and new methodologies means that staying stagnant can quickly make your skills obsolete. Lifelong learning is the key to maintaining relevance, expanding your capabilities, and opening doors to new opportunities.

Why Continuous Learning is Critical

The modern workplace demands adaptability. Roles that didn't exist a decade ago, such as social media manager or data scientist, are now crucial to many businesses. As industries continue to evolve, the skills required to succeed within them also change. Professionals who commit to ongoing learning are better equipped to navigate these shifts, making them more competitive and resilient.

Furthermore, continuous learning fuels personal growth. It fosters a mindset of curiosity, innovation, and flexibility—qualities that are increasingly valued in professional settings. By acquiring new knowledge and skills, you can advance professionally and become a better-rounded person.

Digital Learning Platforms: Tools for Modern Education

The rise of digital learning platforms has revolutionized how we acquire new skills. From online courses to webinars and virtual workshops, the options are endless, offering flexibility and accessibility to learners of all backgrounds.

Popular Platforms for Professional Development

- **Coursera:** Offers a wide range of courses from top universities and institutions worldwide, covering everything from data science to personal development.
- **Udemy:** Known for its extensive catalog of courses, often created by industry professionals, Udemy provides practical knowledge in specific areas like marketing, coding, and leadership.
- **LinkedIn Learning:** This platform integrates seamlessly with your LinkedIn profile, offering personalized course recommendations based on your career goals and interests.
- **edX:** A platform that collaborates with universities such as Harvard and MIT, providing access to high-quality courses in a variety of fields.
- **Skillshare:** Focuses on creative skills, including design, writing, and photography, but also offers business-related courses.

Each of these platforms provides certificates upon completion, which can be added to your resume or LinkedIn profile to showcase your commitment to continuous learning.

Staying Current in Your Industry: Navigating Trends and Innovations

In addition to formal learning, staying ahead in your industry requires keeping up with trends and innovations. This proactive approach ensures that you're not just reacting to changes but anticipating them.

Strategies to Stay Informed

- **Industry News and Journals:** Subscribe to industry-specific publications and newsletters to receive regular updates on the latest trends, research, and innovations.
- **Networking:** Engage with professionals in your field through industry events, conferences, and online forums. Conversations with peers can provide insights into emerging trends and practices.
- **Social Media:** Follow industry leaders and organizations on platforms like Twitter and LinkedIn. These channels often serve as real-time sources of news and discussion.
- **Webinars and Podcasts:** Many industry experts share their knowledge through webinars and podcasts. These formats allow you to learn directly from thought leaders without needing to attend in-person events.
- **Professional Associations:** Joining associations related to your industry can provide access to resources, events, and a network of professionals dedicated to staying ahead of the curve.

By combining these strategies, you can ensure that you're not only aware of current trends but also positioning yourself to capitalize on new opportunities as they arise.

Integrating Learning into a Busy Schedule: Strategies for Success

One of the biggest challenges professionals face is finding the time for continuous learning amidst their busy schedules. However, with the right strategies, it's possible to integrate learning into your daily routine without feeling overwhelmed.

Time Management Tips

- **Micro learning:** Break down your learning into small, manageable segments. For instance, watch a short video during your lunch break or read an article while commuting.
- **Set Clear Goals:** Identify what you want to learn and set specific, measurable goals. This focus will help you stay motivated and track your progress.
- **Create a Learning Schedule:** Dedicate specific times during the week for learning activities, whether it's an hour on Sunday afternoon or 15 minutes each morning.
- **Leverage Downtime:** Make the most of your downtime by listening to podcasts or reading articles related to your career.
- **Combine Learning with Work:** Look for opportunities to apply new skills directly to your work. By actively seeking out new knowledge, you demonstrate your commitment to your career and your value to your employer.

By implementing these strategies, you can make continuous learning a regular part of your life, enhancing your career without sacrificing your personal time.

Quick Wins:

- **Enroll in an Online Course:** Choose a course relevant to your current role or future aspirations and start today.
- **Subscribe to Industry Newsletters:** Sign up for at least one industry-specific newsletter to receive regular updates on trends and innovations.

- **Join a Professional Association:** Identify a relevant association and become a member to gain access to resources and networking opportunities.
- **Listen to a Podcast:** Find a podcast related to your field and listen during your next commute or workout.
- **Set a Learning Goal:** Write down one skill you want to develop in the next month and outline the steps you'll take to achieve it.

Conclusion

In today's rapidly evolving world, continuous learning is essential for both personal and professional growth. Relying solely on the skills and knowledge acquired early in your career is no longer sufficient. Embracing lifelong learning enables you to stay ahead in a landscape characterized by technological advancements and shifting industry demands. This ongoing commitment not only enhances your expertise but also fosters innovation, adaptability, and leadership, crucial for thriving in your field.

Beyond career advancement, continuous learning sharpens your mind, broadens your perspective, and cultivates a culture of curiosity and improvement in every aspect of life. With the advent of digital learning platforms, education has become more accessible than ever, offering a wealth of knowledge from leading institutions and professionals worldwide. This accessibility ensures that growth is within reach for everyone, enriching personal fulfillment and contributing meaningfully to both community and industry. By staying committed to learning, you position yourself to not only keep up with changes but to excel and lead confidently into the future.

Worksheet for Chapter 8: Continuous Learning and Staying Ahead of the Curve

A. Identifying Learning Opportunities

1. **What skills or knowledge areas do you need to develop to stay relevant in your field?**
   - Skill/Knowledge Area 1:
   _____
   _____

   - Skill/Knowledge Area 2:
   _____
   _____

2. **Which resources (e.g., courses, books, and webinars) can help you acquire these skills?**
   - Resource 1:
   _____
   _____

   - Resource 2:
   _____
   _____

3. **Who are the experts or mentors in your industry that you can learn from?**
   - Expert/Mentor 1:
   _____
   _____

   - Expert/Mentor 2:
   _____
   _____

B. Creating a Learning Plan

1. What learning goals do you want to achieve in the next 6 months?
   o Goal 1:
   _____
   _____

   o Goal 2:
   _____
   _____

2. How much time can you realistically dedicate to learning each week?
   o _____

3. Which learning platforms or methods (e.g., online courses, podcasts, and conferences) will you use?
   o Platform/Method 1:
   _____
   _____

   o Platform/Method 2:
   _____
   _____

C. Applying What You've Learned

1. How can you apply new skills or knowledge to your current role or projects?
   o _____
   o _____

2. Who in your organization or network can you share your new insights with?
    - Contact 1: _____

    - Contact 2: _____

3. What projects or tasks can you take on to practice and solidify your new skills?
    - Project/Task 1: _____

    - Project/Task 2: _____

D. Staying Updated in Your Industry

1. Which industry trends or advancements should you keep an eye on?
    - Trend/Advancement 1: _____

    - Trend/Advancement 2: _____

2. What strategies will you use to stay informed about these trends (e.g., newsletters, networking events)?
    - Strategy 1: _____

- Strategy 2:
  _____
  _____

3. **How often will you review and update your learning plan to align with industry changes?**
   - _____

E. Creating CLEAR Learning Goals

1. **Collaborative:** How will you involve peers or mentors in your learning journey?
   - _____
2. **Limited:** What specific learning activities will you focus on this quarter?
   - Activity 1:
     _____
     _____
   - Activity 2:
     _____
     _____
3. **Emotional:** How does continuous learning contribute to your personal and professional growth?
   - _____
4. **Appreciable:** What milestones will indicate your learning progress?
   - Milestone 1:
     _____
     _____
   - Milestone 2:
     _____
     _____

5. **Refinable:** How will you adjust your learning plan if certain goals become irrelevant or unachievable?
    - _____
    - _____

F. Tracking Your Progress

1. **Monthly Review:** What new skills or knowledge have you acquired this month?
    - _____
    - _____
2. **Next Steps:** What will you do next to continue your learning journey?
    - _____
    - _____

Chapter 9: Balancing Work and Life – Maximizing Productivity

Understanding Work-Life Balance

In today's fast-paced world, the concept of work-life balance is often discussed but seldom truly understood. For many, balancing professional responsibilities with personal life seems like an elusive goal, especially in an age where technology has blurred the lines between work and home. The key to achieving a healthy work-life balance lies in understanding that it's not about equally dividing time between work and personal activities. Instead, it's about ensuring that neither domain overpowers the other, allowing you to thrive in both spheres without sacrificing your well-being.

Work-life balance is not a one-size-fits-all concept. Your career goals are personal and can change as your life and career progress. What matters most is finding a rhythm that works for you—a rhythm that allows you to be productive at work while also enjoying a fulfilling personal life.

Managing time, setting limits, and taking care of yourself are key to achieving work-life balance. When these elements are in place, you can reduce stress, prevent burnout, and maintain long-term productivity and satisfaction in both your professional and personal life.

Productivity Tools and Techniques

Maximizing productivity while maintaining work-life balance hinges on your ability to manage time effectively and use the right tools. Here are some productivity techniques and tools that can help:

1. **Time Blocking:** Divide and conquer! Schedule your time effectively. By scheduling work tasks, personal activities, and breaks, you can ensure that both areas of your life receive the attention they need.
2. **The Eisenhower Matrix:** This is a time management tool that helps you prioritize tasks based on urgency and importance. By organizing your tasks, you can concentrate on what's most important in both your work and personal life.
3. **Digital Productivity Tools:** Apps like Trello, Asana, and Todoist can help you organize tasks, set deadlines, and collaborate with others. For personal activities, apps like Habitica or Forest can help you stay on track with personal goals and routines.
4. **The Pomodoro Technique:** This involves working in focused intervals (usually 25 minutes) followed by short breaks. It helps maintain focus and prevent burnout by giving your brain regular rest periods.
5. **Mindfulness and Meditation Apps:** Tools like Headspace and Calm can help you manage stress and stay centered, ensuring that you approach both work and life with a clear, focused mind.

Sustainable Career Growth

Balancing work and life isn't just about managing time; it's about ensuring that your career growth is sustainable. Rapid career advancement can be exciting, but if it comes at the expense of your health, relationships, or personal fulfillment, it's not sustainable in the long run. Here are some strategies to grow your career sustainably:

1. **Set Realistic Goals:** Ambitious goals are important, but they should be realistic and achievable. Setting overly aggressive targets can lead to stress and burnout. Instead, focus on steady, incremental progress.
2. **Prioritize Self-Care:** Regular exercise, healthy eating, and adequate sleep are essential for staying energized and focused. Self-care isn't a luxury; it's a necessity for long-term success.
3. **Continuous Learning:** Invest in your personal and professional development by learning new skills and staying updated with industry trends. This not only helps you stay competitive but also ensures that your career growth aligns with the evolving demands of your field.
4. **Delegate and Outsource:** Delegate tasks or outsource work to others to lighten your workload.
5. Delegating tasks at work and outsourcing certain personal chores can free up time and reduce stress.
6. **Maintain a Support System:** A strong support system, including family, friends, and mentors, is vital. They can offer advice, encouragement, and a sense of balance when work pressures mount.
7. **Reflect and Adjust:** Periodically evaluate your work-life balance and make necessary changes. Life is dynamic, and your approach to balancing work and life should be flexible enough to adapt to changes.

Case Study 1: Alara's Journey to Reclaiming Work-Life Balance

Background:
Alara is a senior project manager at a fast-paced tech company. She recently received a promotion, which significantly increased her workload. Despite her career success, Alara found herself constantly exhausted, missing

out on family time, and feeling overwhelmed by the demands of her job. Her work-life balance was virtually non-existent, leading to increased stress and a sense of burnout.

Challenges:
Alara struggled with setting boundaries between work and personal life. Her workdays often extended into the evening, and she found it difficult to disconnect from work emails and tasks, even on weekends. The pressure to perform at a high level in her new role left her with little time for self-care or family activities.

Solution:
To address her work-life imbalance, Alara implemented several strategies:

- **Time Blocking**: Alara started time-blocking her days, designating specific hours for work, family, and personal activities. She used her calendar to ensure she adhered to these blocks.
- **Setting Boundaries**: She established a firm end to her workday at 6 PM and turned off work-related notifications after that time. Weekends were reserved for family and relaxation.
- **Prioritizing Self-Care**: Alara incorporated daily exercise and mindfulness practices into her routine, which helped her manage stress and stay focused.

Outcome:
After a few weeks, Alara noticed significant improvements in her energy levels and overall well-being. She was able to maintain her productivity at work without sacrificing her personal life. Her relationships with family members improved, and she felt more present and engaged in her personal life. By setting clear boundaries and prioritizing

self-care, Alara successfully reclaimed her work-life balance.

Case Study 2: Ester's Strategy for Sustainable Career Growth

Background:
Ester is a mid-level marketing professional who has been rapidly climbing the corporate ladder. While his career was advancing quickly, Ester began experiencing severe burnout due to the constant pressure to meet high expectations. He often sacrificed personal time to take on additional projects, leading to chronic stress and health issues.

Challenges:
Ester's ambition led him to take on more work than he could handle. He neglected self-care, resulting in poor sleep, weight gain, and increased anxiety. The lack of balance between his career and personal life was unsustainable, and his performance at work began to suffer as a result.

Solution:
Ester decided to take a step back and reassess his approach:

- **Setting Realistic Goals**: Ester revised his career goals, setting more realistic and achievable targets. He focused on steady progress rather than rapid advancement.
- **Delegating Tasks**: He learned to delegate responsibilities to his team members, which lightened his workload and allowed him to focus on high-priority tasks.
- **Investing in Self-Care**: Ester made significant lifestyle changes, including a healthier diet, regular

exercise, and sufficient sleep. He also started practicing mindfulness to manage stress.

Outcome:
By making these adjustments, Ester was able to maintain his career momentum without compromising his health and well-being. His productivity improved, and he felt more fulfilled both personally and professionally. Ester's story highlights the importance of setting realistic goals and prioritizing self-care for sustainable career growth.

Case Study 3: Emily's Quest for Work-Life Harmony as a Working Mother

Background:
Emily is a marketing director and a mother of two young children. After returning from maternity leave, Emily found it challenging to balance her demanding job with her responsibilities at home. The constant juggling act left her feeling guilty for not being fully present either at work or with her family.

Challenges:
Emily's biggest challenge was time management. She struggled to meet the demands of her job while ensuring she was there for her children. The guilt of not spending enough time with her family affected her performance at work, and she often felt overwhelmed.

Solution:
Emily used these methods to take back control of her situation:

- **Flexible Work Schedule**: Emily negotiated a more flexible work schedule with her employer, allowing her to start and finish work earlier in the day, giving her more time with her children in the evening.

- **Prioritizing Tasks**: She adopted the Eisenhower Matrix to prioritize her work tasks, focusing on what was most urgent and important. This helped her organize her tasks more efficiently.
- **Support System**: Emily enlisted the help of her spouse and extended family to share parenting responsibilities. This support allowed her to focus on her work when needed without feeling guilty.

Outcome:
With these changes, Emily achieved a better balance between her work and family life. Her performance at work improved, and she felt more present and engaged with her children. Emily's case demonstrates how flexible work arrangements and a strong support system can play a crucial role in achieving work-life harmony.

Quick Wins

To help you start balancing work and life effectively while maximizing productivity, here are some quick wins:

1. **Start Time Blocking Today:** Choose a digital or physical calendar and begin time-blocking your day. Make sure your schedule includes tasks for work, personal life, and rest.
2. **Prioritize with the Eisenhower Matrix:** Categorize tasks by urgency and importance, and focus on the most critical ones.
3. **Use a Productivity App:** Download a productivity app like Todoist or Trello and start organizing your tasks. Set deadlines and prioritize.

4. **Practice Mindfulness:** Spend 5 minutes today using a mindfulness app like Headspace. Concentrate on your breath and let go of your thoughts.
5. **Set Boundaries:** Define a clear end to your workday. Turn off work notifications and focus on your personal life after work hours.
6. **Delegate One Task:** Identify one work task or personal chore that you can delegate or outsource today.
7. **Reflect on Your Day:** Before going to bed, reflect on your day's balance. Did you give enough attention to both work and life? Make a note of one thing you can improve tomorrow.

Conclusion

Maintaining a healthy work-life balance while maximizing productivity is a continuous process that requires intentional effort and flexibility. By implementing the strategies and techniques outlined in this chapter, you can create a sustainable routine that supports both your career ambitions and personal well-being. Remember, the goal is not perfection but a harmonious balance that allows you to thrive both professionally and personally. With the right mindset, tools, and practices, you can achieve a fulfilling and productive life.

Worksheet for Chapter 9: Balancing Work and Life – Maximizing Productivity

A. Assessing Your Current Work-Life Balance

1. **On a scale of 1 to 10, how would you rate your current work-life balance?**
   - _____

2. **What areas of your life (e.g., family, health, and hobbies) need more attention?**
   - Area 1:
     _____
     _____
   - Area 2:
     _____
     _____

3. **What aspects of your work are taking up the most time or causing stress?**
   - Aspect 1:
     _____
     _____
   - Aspect 2:
     _____
     _____

B. Setting CLEAR Goals for Work-Life Balance

1. **Collaborative:** Who can you collaborate with (e.g., colleagues, family) to achieve a better work-life balance?
   - _____
   - _____

2. **Limited:** What specific activities or tasks will you limit to free up time for personal life?
    - Task/Activity 1:

      _____

      _____

    - Task/Activity 2:

      _____

      _____

3. **Emotional:** How does achieving a better work-life balance make you feel?
    - _____
    - _____

4. **Appreciable:** What small changes can you implement immediately to improve your balance?
    - Change 1:

      _____

      _____

    - Change 2:

      _____

      _____

5. **Refinable:** How will you adjust your balance plan as your personal and professional circumstances change?
    - _____
    - _____

C. Time Management Strategies

1. **What time management techniques (e.g., Pomodoro, time blocking) will you use to manage your work tasks more efficiently?**

- Technique 1:
  _____
  _____

- Technique 2:
  _____
  _____

2. How will you prioritize tasks to ensure you're focusing on the most important work first?
   - _____
   - _____

3. How much time will you allocate daily or weekly for personal activities?
   - _____
   - _____

D. Setting Boundaries

1. What boundaries will you set to protect your personal time (e.g., no work emails after 7 PM)?
   - Boundary 1:
     _____
     _____
   - Boundary 2:
     _____
     _____

2. How will you communicate these boundaries to your colleagues or clients?
   - _____
   - _____

3. What strategies will you use to enforce these boundaries consistently?
   - _____
   - _____

E. Self-Care and Recharging

1. What self-care activities will you incorporate into your routine to maintain your well-being?
   - Activity 1:
     _____

   - Activity 2:
     _____

2. How often will you schedule time for relaxation or hobbies?
   - _____

3. What signs of burnout will you watch for, and how will you address them if they arise?
   - _____
   - _____

F. Monitoring Your Progress

1. **Weekly Review:** How balanced was your work and personal life this week? What worked well, and what didn't?
   - _____
   - _____

2. **Next Steps:** What adjustments will you make next week to improve your balance?

    o _____
    o _____

Chapter 10: Measuring Progress and Building Your Career Legacy

Defining Success: Beyond Traditional Metrics

Success is subjective and has traditionally been measured by material achievements. While these are important, they don't capture the full picture of a fulfilling career. This chapter is about expanding the definition of success to include personal fulfillment, ethical behavior, and the long-term impact you leave on your industry and community.

The Multiple Facets of Success

To begin, consider the different aspects of success:

- **Personal Fulfillment:** Are you satisfied with the work you do daily? Does it align with your values and passions? Personal fulfillment is about finding joy and purpose in your work, ensuring it contributes positively to your overall well-being.
- **Ethical Behavior:** Your career legacy isn't just about what you achieve but how you achieve it. Acting with integrity, making decisions that are morally sound, and maintaining professionalism are all critical components of a successful career.
- **Long-Term Impact:** Think about the legacy you want to leave behind. This might involve mentoring others, contributing to your field's body of knowledge, or making a positive difference in your community. The impact you make can be as significant as any title or award.

Tools for Progress Tracking

Once you've defined what success means to you, the next step is tracking your progress. This isn't just about ticking off boxes on a to-do list but involves deeper reflection on how far you've come and where you're heading.

Progress Tracking Tools

1. **Journaling:** Regularly write about your achievements, challenges, and learnings. This helps in reflecting on your journey and identifying patterns in your growth.
2. **SMART Goals:** While traditional, SMART goals (Specific, Measurable, Achievable, Relevant, Time-bound) remain an effective way to set and measure progress.
3. **Career Dashboard:** Use tools like spreadsheets or dedicated apps to track key milestones, skill development, and networking efforts. This gives you a visual representation of your progress.
4. **Mentor Feedback:** Regular check-ins with a mentor can provide an external perspective on your progress and offer valuable advice for continued growth.

Building Your Career Legacy

Your career legacy is the lasting impression you leave on your industry, colleagues, and community. It's about more than just what you achieve; it's about how others perceive your contributions and character.

Steps to Building a Legacy

1. **Identify Your Core Values:** Start by understanding what values are most important to you. These will guide your decisions and actions throughout your career.
2. **Contribute Beyond Your Role:** Seek opportunities to mentor others, lead initiatives, or volunteer for causes related to your industry. This helps create a long-term and significant effect.
3. **Maintain Professional Relationships:** Strong, meaningful relationships are a significant part of any legacy. Keep in touch with your network, offer help when needed, and remain supportive of others' successes.
4. **Be Consistent:** Your legacy is built over time through consistent actions and behaviors. Stay true to your values, maintain high standards of integrity, and continually strive to contribute positively.

Reflection Exercises: Looking Back and Forward

Reflecting on your experiences can help you grow personally and professionally. It allows you to assess your journey, learn from experiences, and plan for the future. Use the following exercises to help you reflect on your career path:

Reflection Exercises

1. **Past Achievements and Learnings:** Reflect on your significant achievements and the lessons learned from past challenges. What do you wish you could have done differently

2. **Current Satisfaction Levels:** Evaluate your current satisfaction with your career. Are you fulfilled? Are there areas of your life where you feel stuck or unsatisfied?
3. **Future Aspirations:** Think about where you want to be in the next 5-10 years. What do you need to change or improve to reach those goals?
4. **Legacy Vision:** Write down what you want your career legacy to be. How do you hope others will remember you in your career?

Quick Wins

1. **Create a Personal Success Definition:** Take some time to define what success means to you, beyond just professional achievements.
2. **Start a Career Journal:** Begin documenting your career journey, focusing on milestones, learnings, and reflections.
3. **Reach Out to a Mentor:** Set up a meeting with a mentor to discuss your progress and gain insights on your career trajectory.
4. **Identify Legacy Opportunities:** Look for ways to contribute to your industry or community that align with your values and long-term goals.
5. **Reflect Weekly:** Set aside 15 minutes each week to reflect on your achievements, challenges, and what you've learned.

Conclusion

Building a successful career goes beyond simply achieving goals or advancing up the corporate ladder. It's about crafting a legacy that mirrors your core values, leaves a positive impact on others, and brings deep personal fulfillment. Success is not a one-size-fits-all concept; it's about defining what success truly means to you and ensuring that your professional journey aligns with your broader life goals. By consciously reflecting on your values, setting meaningful milestones, and regularly tracking your progress, you can build a career that is not only successful in traditional terms but also rich with purpose and satisfaction.

Whether you're just beginning your career or are already well-established, it's never too late to redefine what success looks like for you and to start building a legacy that resonates with who you are. This process involves intentionality in your daily actions, cultivating relationships that matter, and making decisions that reflect the impact you want to leave behind. By focusing on legacy-building, you ensure that your career contributes not only to your personal growth and success but also to the betterment of those around you, leaving a lasting, meaningful imprint on your professional landscape.

Worksheet for Chapter 10: Building a Lasting Legacy – Making an Impact That Endures

A. Defining Your Legacy

1. **What do you want to be remembered for in your personal and professional life?**
   - Personal Legacy:
     _____
     _____
   - Professional Legacy:
     _____
     _____

2. **What values and principles are most important to you and should be reflected in your legacy?**
   - Value 1:
     _____
     _____
   - Value 2:
     _____
     _____

3. **Who are the key people or groups you want to impact through your legacy?**
   - Person/Group 1:
     _____
     _____
   - Person/Group 2:
     _____
     _____

B. Setting CLEAR Goals for Your Legacy

1. **Collaborative:** Who can you collaborate with to build and sustain your legacy?
    - _____

2. **Limited:** What specific focus areas will you limit your efforts to ensure a meaningful and manageable impact?
    - Focus Area 1:
      _____
      _____
    - Focus Area 2:
      _____
      _____

3. **Emotional:** How does the thought of building a legacy make you feel?
    - _____

4. **Appreciable:** What small, tangible actions can you take now to start building your legacy?
    - Action 1:
      _____
      _____
    - Action 2:
      _____
      _____

5. **Refinable:** How will you refine and adapt your legacy plan as you grow and evolve?
    - _____
    - _____

C. Creating Impact in Your Personal Life

1. How will you positively influence your family and friends?
    - _____

2. What traditions or practices will you establish to pass on your values to future generations?
    - Tradition 1:
      _____
      _____
    - Tradition 2:
      _____
      _____

3. How will you support your community and contribute to causes you care about?
    - _____
    - _____

D. Creating Impact in Your Professional Life

1. What contributions do you want to make to your industry or field?
    - Contribution 1:
      _____
      _____
    - Contribution 2:
      _____
      _____

2. How will you mentor or support others in your profession?

o
   o

3. What innovations or changes do you want to drive that will leave a lasting mark?
   o
   o

E. Sustaining Your Legacy Over Time

1. What ongoing actions will you take to ensure your legacy endures?
   o   Action 1:
   _____
   _____

   o   Action 2:
   _____
   _____

2. How will you pass on your knowledge and experiences to others?
   o
   o

3. What will you do to maintain alignment between your daily actions and your long-term legacy goals?
   o
   o

F. Reflecting on Your Legacy

1. How often will you review and reflect on your legacy plan to ensure it remains relevant?
    o _____

2. What indicators will you use to measure the impact you're having?
    o   Indicator 1:
    _____
    _____

    o   Indicator 2:
    _____
    _____

3. What will success look like for your legacy?
    o _____
    o _____

www.ingramcontent.com/pod-product-compliance
Lightning Source LLC
Chambersburg PA
CBHW050312230526
45471CB00005B/2142